Reading Together

Night-night, Knight

And Other Poems

Read it together

Night-night, Knight is a collection of rhymes and playful tongue twisters that Michael Rosen has put together especially for this book.

Some of the rhymes may be very familiar, some are humorous versions of traditional rhymes and some will be completely new to both you and your child. There is plenty to talk about and much to enjoy saying out aloud.

Reading rhymes aloud to children makes joining in a natural way to take on the reading. Try leaving a space at the end of a line for your child to finish.

If children hear the rhymes read again and again, they are sure to develop favourites and begin to retell or re-read these by themselves. They may not always match the words on the page exactly at first. This takes time and confidence.

Granny Granny
please comb my hair
you always take your time
you always take such care

I like bru
better t
combs

I can put my socks on,
I can find my vest,
I can put my pants on –

I can't do the rest
I can really!

I'm a tig
With stripy
Don't come
Or I'll go G

If your child gets stuck on a word, help them to guess what it says by looking at the pictures or the letter the word begins with, or by finishing the rhyme and then coming back to it. With a longer word, it can help to break it down into meaningful chunks.

> *I am running in a circle and my feet are getting sore, and my head is sp–*

I am running in a circle
and my feet are getting sore,
and my head is
spin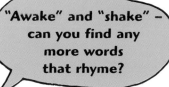

> **If I cover the ending, what does it say?**

> ...ning" and "warning" ...ound the same.

> **"Awake" and "shake" – can you find any more words that rhyme?**

Rhyme encourages children to look closely at the words and letters and listen to the sounds of words. It also helps children to notice word patterns and to play with language.

> **I wouldn't run away with the spoon. I'd run away with the chocolate biscuits.**

Some of the poems in this book are different versions of well-known rhymes. Children will enjoy talking about these differences and may try making up their own versions.

We hope you enjoy reading this book together.

For Caroline, Kaz and Clare
S.H.

First published 1998 by Walker Books Ltd
87 Vauxhall Walk, London SE11 5HJ

This edition produced 2002 for
The Book People Ltd, Hall Wood Avenue,
Haydock, St Helens WA11 9UL

10 9 8 7 6 5 4 3 2 1

ISBN 0-7445-4884-5

The editor and publisher gratefully acknowledge permission to
reproduce the following copyright material:

John Agard: "So-So Joe" from No Hickory, No Dickory, No Dock
published by Viking 1991 and "Where Does Laughter Begin?" from
Laughter Is an Egg published by Viking 1990, reprinted by kind
permission of John Agard c/o Caroline Sheldon Literary Agency.
Tony Bradman: "I Can Put My Socks On" from A Kiss on the Nose,
reprinted by permission of William Heinemann. Richard Edwards:
"How?" from The Word Party published by Puffin 1987, reprinted by
permission of the author. Eleanor Farjeon: "Cats" from The Children's
Bells, reprinted by permission of David Higham Associates.
Michelle Magorian: "I Won't" from Waiting for My Shorts to Dry
published by Viking Kestrel 1989 © Michelle Magorian 1989, reprinted
by permission of Frederick Warne & Co. Spike Milligan: "Today I Saw a
Little Worm" © Spike Milligan 1959, 1961, 1963, reprinted by
permission of Spike Milligan Productions Ltd.

Grace Nichols: "Granny, Granny, Please Comb My Hair" from Come
On into My Tropical Garden published by A & C Black, reprinted by
permission of Curtis Brown Ltd., on behalf of Grace Nichols © 1988.
Jack Prelutsky: "I Am Running in a Circle" from New Kid on the Block,
reprinted by permission of William Heinemann Ltd. Michael Rosen:
"Nursery Crimes" © Michael Rosen 1985, reprinted by permission of
André Deutsch Children's Books, an imprint of Scholastic Ltd. Clive
Sansom: "The Dustman" from Speech Rhymes, reprinted by permission
of A & C Black Ltd. Ian Serraillier: "The Tickle Rhyme" from The
Monster Horse © 1950 published by Oxford University Press, reprinted
by permission of Anne Serraillier.

While every effort has been made to obtain permission, there may still
be cases in which we have failed to trace a copyright holder, and we
would like to apologize for any apparent negligence.

Night-night, Knight
And Other Poems

Chosen by **Michael Rosen**
Illustrated by **Sue Heap**

TED SMART

So-So Joe

So-So Joe
de so-so man
wore a so-so suit
with a so-so shoe.
So-So Joe
de so-so man
lived in a so-so house
with a so-so view.
And when you asked So-So Joe
de so-so man
How do you do?
So-So Joe
de so-so man
would say to you:
Just so-so
Nothing new.

John Agard

Fire

Fire! Fire!
said Mrs Dyer;
Where? Where?
said Mrs Dare;
Up the town,
said Mrs Brown;
Any damage?
said Mrs Gamage;
None at all,
said Mrs Hall.

The Dustman

Every Thursday morning,
Before you're quite awake,
Without the slightest warning
The house begins to shake
With a Biff! ... Bang!
Biff! Bang! Bash!

It's the dustman, who begins
(Bang! ... Crash!)
To empty both the bins
Of their rubbish and their ash,
With a Biff! ... Bang!
Biff! Bang! Bash!

Clive Sansom

The Key of the Kingdom

This is the key of the kingdom:
In that kingdom is a city,
In that city is a town,
In that town there is a street,
In that street there winds a lane,
In that lane there is a yard,
In that yard there is a house,
In that house there waits a room,
In that room there is a bed,
On that bed there is a basket,
A basket of flowers.

Flowers in the basket,
Basket on the bed,
Bed in the room,
Room in the house,
House in the weedy yard,
Yard in the winding lane,
Lane in the broad street,
Street in the high town,
Town in the city,
City in the kingdom:
This is the key of the kingdom.

Lane

Granny Granny Please Comb My Hair

Granny Granny
please comb my hair
you always take your time
you always take such care

You put me to sit on a cushion
between your knees
you rub a little coconut oil
parting gentle as a breeze

Mummy Mummy
she's always in a hurry-hurry
rush
she pulls my hair
sometimes she tugs

But Granny
you have all the time in the world
and when you're finished
you always turn my head and say
"Now who's a nice girl".

Grace Nichols

After a Bath

After my bath
I try, try, try
to wipe myself
till I'm dry, dry, dry.

Hands to wipe
and fingers and toes
and two wet legs
and a shiny nose.

Just think how much
less time I'd take
if I were a dog
and could shake, shake, shake.

Aileen Fisher

I Can Put My Socks On

I can put my socks on,
I can find my vest,
I can put my pants on –
I can't do the rest.

Tony Bradman

There Was a Young Lady Named Maggie

There was a young lady named Maggie,
Whose dog was enormous and shaggy.
    The front end of him
    Looked vicious and grim,
But the back end was friendly and waggy.

A Cheerful Old Bear at the Zoo

A cheerful old bear at the zoo,
Could always find something to do.
    When it bored him to go
    On a walk to and fro,
He reversed it and walked fro and to.

There Was a Young Farmer of Leeds

There was a young farmer of Leeds,
Who swallowed six packets of seeds.
    It soon came to pass
    He was covered with grass,
And he couldn't sit down for the weeds.

There Was a Young Man of Devizes

There was a young man of Devizes,
Whose ears were of different sizes.
    One was so small
    It was no use at all,
But the other was huge and won prizes.

I Won't

I won't, no I won't, no I won't do that.
I don't want to, I don't have to,
No I won't wear that hat.

I hate it, yes I hate it, yes I hate, hate, hate.
You can't make me, I don't want to,
I don't care if we are late.

Yes I'm naughty, yes I'm naughty,
Yes I know, know, know.
But I won't wear that hat
So it's No! No! No!

Michelle Magorian

Overheard on a Saltmarsh

Nymph, nymph, what are your beads?
Green glass, goblin. Why do you stare at them?
Give them me.
        No.
Give them me. Give them me.
        No.
Then I will howl all night in the reeds,
Lie in the mud and howl for them.
Goblin, why do you love them so?
They are better than stars or water,
Better than voices of winds that sing,
Better than any man's fair daughter,
Your green glass beads on a silver ring.

Hush, I stole them out of the moon.
Give me your beads, I desire them.
        No.
I will howl in a deep lagoon
For your green glass beads, I love them so.
Give them me. Give them.
        No.

Harold Munro

Swan, Swim over the Sea

Swan, swim over the sea.
Swim, swan, swim!
Swan, swim back again.
Well swum, swan!

"Night-night, Knight,"

"Night-night, Knight," said one Knight
to the other Knight the other night.
"Night-night, Knight."

Peter Piper Picked a Peck of Pickled Pepper

Peter Piper picked a peck of pickled pepper,
A peck of pickled pepper Peter Piper picked.
If Peter Piper picked a peck of pickled pepper,
Where's the peck of pickled pepper Peter Piper picked?

You can have

Fried fresh fish,

Fish fried fresh,

Fresh fried fish,

Fresh fish fried,

Or fish fresh fried.

Cats

Cats sleep
Anywhere,
Any table,
Any chair,
Top of piano,
Window-ledge,
In the middle,
On the edge,
Open drawer,
Empty shoe,
Anybody's
Lap will do,
Fitted in a
Cardboard box,
In the cupboard
With your frocks –
Anywhere!
They don't care!
Cats sleep
Anywhere.

Eleanor Farjeon

Tiger

I'm a tiger
Striped with fur
Don't come near
Or I might Grrr
Don't come near
Or I might growl
Don't come near
Or I might
BITE!

Mary Ann Hoberman

I Am Running in a Circle

I am running in a circle
and my feet are getting sore,
and my head is
spinning
spinning
as it's never spun before,
I am
dizzy
dizzy
dizzy.

Oh! I cannot bear much more,
I am trapped in a
revolving
...volving
...volving
...volving door!

Jack Prelutsky

NURSERY CRIMES by Michael Rosen

Hush-a-bye, Gravy, on the Tree Top

Hush-a-bye, gravy, on the tree top,
When the wind blows the ladle will rock;
When the bough breaks the ladle will fall,
Down will come gravy, ladle and all.

Humpty Dumpty Sat on the Wall

Humpty Dumpty sat on the wall,
Humpty Dumpty had a great fall;
All the King's horses and all the King's men
Trod on him.

Hey Diddle, Diddle

Hey diddle, diddle,
The cat and the fiddle,
The cow jumped over the moon;
The little dog laughed
To see such fun,
And the dish ran away with the chocolate biscuits.

Today I Saw a Little Worm

Today I saw a little worm
Wriggling on his belly.
Perhaps he'd like to come inside
And see what's on the telly.

Spike Milligan

"Who's That Tickling My Back?"
"Who's that tickling my back?"
Said the wall.
"Me," said the caterpillar.
"I'm learning to crawl."   *Ian Serraillier*

Where Does Laughter Begin?

Does it start in your head
and spread to your toe?

Does it start in your cheeks
and grow downward so
till your knees feel weak?

Does it start with a tickle
in your tummy so
till you want to jump right out

of all your skin?
Or does laughter simply begin

with your mouth?

John Agard

Questions at Night

Why
Is the sky?

What starts the thunder overhead?
Who makes the crashing noise?
Are the angels falling out of bed?
Are they breaking all their toys?

Why does the sun go down so soon?
Why do the night-clouds crawl
Hungrily up to the new-laid moon
And swallow it, shell and all?

If there's a Bear among the stars,
As all the people say,
Won't he jump over those pasture-bars
And drink up the Milky Way?

Does every star that happens to fall
Turn into a firefly?
Can't it ever get back to Heaven at all?
And why
Is the sky?

Louis Untermeyer

How?

How did the sun get up in the sky?
– A billy goat tossed it up too high,
Said my uncle.

How did the stars get up there too?
– They're sparks from the thunder-horse's shoe,
Said my uncle.

And tell me about the moon as well.
– The moon jumped out of an oyster shell,
Said my uncle.

And how did the oceans get so deep?
– I'll tell you tomorrow. Now go to sleep,
Said my uncle.

Richard Edwards

Silverly

Silverly,
     Silverly
Over the
     Trees,
The moon drifts
     By on a
Runaway
     Breeze.

Dozily,
     Dozily
Deep in her
     Bed,
A little girl
     Dreams with the
Moon in her
     Head.

Dennis Lee

Read it again

Learn a poem

Children can learn a favourite poem by heart if they hear and read it again and again. They might be encouraged to act it out for you with simple props or to tape it with sound effects and simple musical instruments.

The other was huge and won prizes.

"Who's that tickling my back?" Said the wall.

"Me," said the caterpillar...

Play-reading

It can be fun to read a poem by passing it between adult and child, like reading a play. Good poems for this are *Overheard on a Saltmarsh*, *Who's That Tickling My Back?*, *Fire* and *How?*

Collecting poems

Your child can select their favourite poem to illustrate, using a large sheet of paper. They could copy out the poem, perhaps with your help, and stick it on the wall.

A cheerful old bear at the ZOO
Couldalways find some-
thing to do:
When it bored him
to go
On a walk to
and
fro
He reversed
it and
walked
fro and
to.

Make a collection

You could also put together a collection of your child's favourite poems and rhymes in a little book. These can be illustrated and read time and time again.

Play the poem game

Who wore a so-so shoe?

Who's always in a hurry-hurry?

Who swallowed six packets of seeds?

Who wants the green glass beads?

Who picked a peck of pickled pepper?

Where do cats sleep?

Who ran away with the chocolate biscuits?

Who tossed the sun up in the sky?

Where did the swan swim?

You and your child can play the poem game and test your knowledge of the poems. Take it in turns to choose a square and answer the question. You can check the answers by looking back through the book.